Baboons

Written by
Alexis Roumanis

www.av2books.com

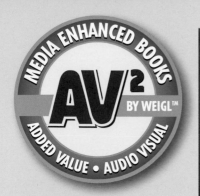

AV² provides enriched content that supplements and complements this book. Weigl's AV² books strive to create inspired learning and engage young minds in a total learning experience.

Your AV² Media Enhanced books come alive with...

Audio
Listen to sections of the book read aloud.

Key Words
Study vocabulary, and complete a matching word activity.

Video
Watch informative video clips.

Quizzes
Test your knowledge.

Go to **www.av2books.com**, and enter this book's unique code.

BOOK CODE

J494795

Embedded Weblinks
Gain additional information for research.

Slide Show
View images and captions, and prepare a presentation.

AV² by Weigl brings you media enhanced books that support active learning.

Try This!
Complete activities and hands-on experiments.

... and much, much more!

Published by AV² by Weigl
350 5th Avenue, 59th Floor
New York, NY 10118
Websites: www.av2books.com   www.weigl.com

Library of Congress Cataloging-in-Publication Data

Roumanis, Alexis.
Baboons/Alexis Roumanis.
    pages cm. -- (Amazing primates)
 Includes index.
ISBN 978-1-4896-2866-4 (hardcover : alk. paper) -- ISBN 978-1-4896-2867-1 (softcover : alk. paper) --
ISBN 978-1-4896-2868-8 (single user ebk.) -- ISBN 978-1-4896-2869-5 (multi user ebk.)
1. Baboons--Juvenile literature. I. Title.
 QL737.P93R68 2014
 599.8'65--dc23

                                2014038981

Printed in the United States of America in Brainerd, Minnesota
1 2 3 4 5 6 7 8 9 0 18 17 16 15 14

122014
WEP081214

Project Coordinator: Katie Gillespie
Art Director: Terry Paulhus

Contents

Meet the Baboon

Baboons are **mammals** that belong to the **order** of **primates**. There are about 300 **species** of primates. Primates range in size from a 1 ounce (30 gram) pygmy mouse lemur to a 400 pound (181 kilogram) gorilla. Baboons can weigh from 33 to 82 pounds (22 to 37 kg).

Baboons live in large groups called troops. There can be as many as 300 baboons in a single troop. Social bonds within troops rely on grooming. To groom, one baboon will remove bugs and **parasites** from another's fur. Troop members can communicate with each other using more than 30 different sounds.

Baboons spend many hours each day grooming each other.

All About
Baboons

Primates include monkeys, apes, and other animals, such as lemurs and lorises. There are about 260 species of monkeys in the world. Scientists divide them up into Old World and New World monkeys.

Old World monkeys live in Africa and Asia. New World monkeys live in South America. Baboons are the largest species of the Old World monkeys. They can be found in central Africa, from Guinea to Somalia, and on the Arabian Peninsula in Yemen and Saudi Arabia.

Like most primates, baboons take good care of their young.

Comparing Primates

Because there are so many species of primates, scientists split them into subgroups. Each of these subgroups is called a superfamily. There are six superfamilies of primates. Grouping primates makes it easier to study their similarities and differences.

Lemurs

+ **Length:**
3.5 to 28 inches
(9 to 71.1 centimeters)
excluding tail
+ **Weight:**
1.1 ounces to 21
pounds (30 g
to 9.5 kg)
+ **Special Feature:**
Lemurs are the primate
at the highest risk
of **extinction**.

Tarsiers

+ **Length:**
3.6 to 6.4 inches
(9.1 to 16.2 cm)
excluding tail
+ **Weight:**
2.8 to 5.8 ounces
(79.3 to 164.4 g)
+ **Special Feature:**
Tarsiers have
the largest eyes,
compared to body
size, of all mammals.

Lorises

+ **Length:**
7.5 to 15 inches
(19 to 38 cm)
+ **Weight:**
9 ounces to 4.6 pounds
(255 g to 2 kg)
+ **Special Feature:**
Lorises are the only
poisonous primate.
They secrete a **toxic**
oil from a gland in
their elbow.

Old World Monkeys

+ **Length:**
13.4 to 37 inches
(34 to 94 cm)
excluding tail
+ **Weight:**
25 ounces to
110 pounds
(700 g to 50 kg)
+ **Special Feature:**
They have nostrils
that are narrow and
point downward.

New World Monkeys

+ **Length:**
5.5 to 28 inches
(14 to 70 cm)
excluding tail
+ **Weight:**
4.2 ounces to
33 pounds
(120 g to 15 kg)
+ **Special Feature:**
They have nostrils
that are broad
and point outward.

Apes

+ **Length:**
3 to 6 feet
(90 cm to 1.8 meters)
+ **Weight:**
12 to 399 pounds
(5 to 181 kg)
+ **Special Feature:**
Apes do not have tails.
They are the most
intelligent of
all primates.

Baboon History

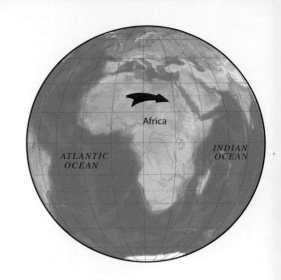

Africa

ATLANTIC OCEAN

INDIAN OCEAN

Baboons originally came from Africa. Nearly 1.8 million years ago, baboons began to spread across the African **continent**. During **glacial periods**, groups of baboons became separated from each other. The different groups developed different **adaptations.** This helped create five different species of baboon. They are chacma, yellow, olive, red Guinea, and hamadryas.

Baboons' main **predators** are people, leopards, and cheetahs. Of the three, people pose the biggest threat. Some people hunt baboons or capture them for medical research. Increases in farmland, **irrigation** projects, and human settlements have also left less land for baboons.

KEEPING SAFE

Baboons take shelter in tall trees or on cliffs to stay safe.

Sometimes, even in trees, baboons are not safe from leopards.

Where Baboons Live

Baboons prefer to live in dry **habitats**, such as **savannas**. Sometimes, they live in tropical forests. Baboons spend most of their time on land, and very little time in trees. In the mornings and afternoons, they travel large distances in search of food.

The place where baboons roam and hunt is called a territory. A troop can have a territory that is around 25 square miles (40 square kilometers). Troops do not mark their territories like some animals do. They use vocalizations, such as barks or screams, and **visual displays** to keep other troops away. Different troops will usually leave each other alone. However, sometimes a group of young males will attack a troop to steal their females.

A troop can be made up of 5 to 300 baboons.

Baboons always try to find shelter near a source of water.

Baboons are very smart. Their brains
are large in relation to their body size.
Scientists believe that brain size of
primates is related to the size of the groups
in which they live. Primates that live in large
groups, such as baboons, develop
new ways to cooperate and
communicate. This is
believed to encourage
brain growth.

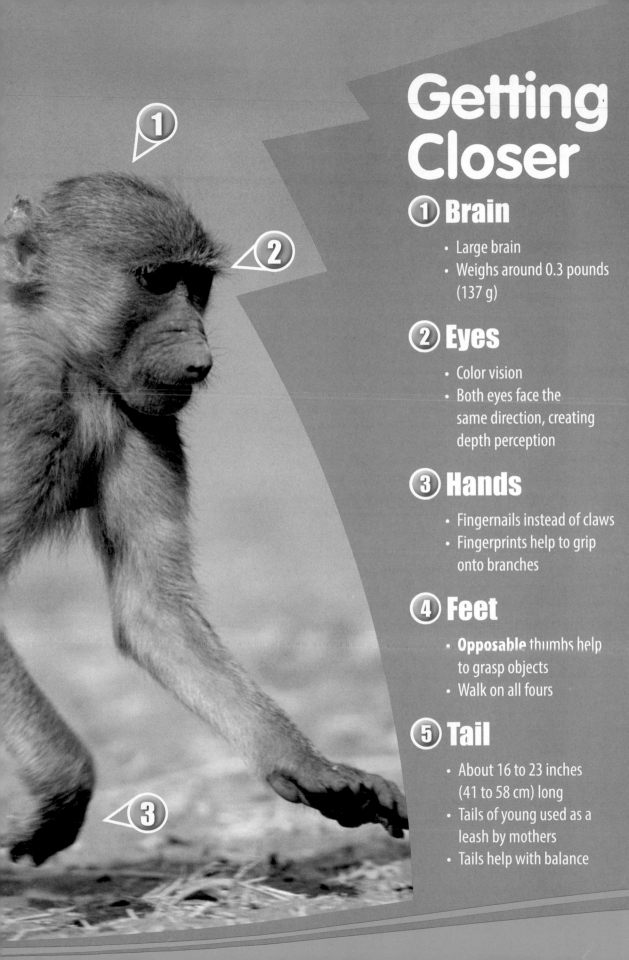

Getting Closer

① Brain
- Large brain
- Weighs around 0.3 pounds (137 g)

② Eyes
- Color vision
- Both eyes face the same direction, creating depth perception

③ Hands
- Fingernails instead of claws
- Fingerprints help to grip onto branches

④ Feet
- **Opposable** thumbs help to grasp objects
- Walk on all fours

⑤ Tail
- About 16 to 23 inches (41 to 58 cm) long
- Tails of young used as a leash by mothers
- Tails help with balance

What Do Baboons Eat?

Like most primates, baboons are omnivores, meaning they eat both plants and animals. They will climb trees to eat fruit, leaves, and bark. Baboons will also dig holes to find roots and insects.

Both male and female baboons will hunt young mammals, lizards, and even turtles. To find **prey**, baboons wave their arms through tall grasses as they walk. This can cause prey to run, making it easier for baboons to see them. Baboons will also hunt in a large group to take down bigger mammals. These groups have been known to attack young gazelles.

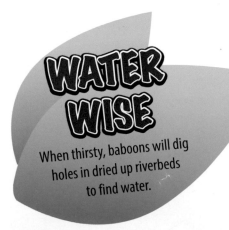

WATER WISE

When thirsty, baboons will dig holes in dried up riverbeds to find water.

Baboons have cheek pouches where they store food, similar to hamsters.

Baboon Life Cycle

Baboons do not have a mating season. They can mate at any time of the year. Female baboons can mate when they are five years of age. Males are ready to mate when they are between seven and ten years old. Infants are born about 170 days after mating.

Birth to 3 Weeks

Infants are not able to walk for the first few weeks. They are born with a strong grip. This helps them to cling onto their mother's belly while she looks for food. Newborn infants weigh around 2.5 pounds (1 kg).

Most baboons give birth at night. The mother uses her teeth to cut the **umbilical cord**. Then, she cleans the infant. Baboons usually have only one baby at a time. Twins are very rare. Females give birth about once every two years.

4 Years and Older

Males leave their troop at around four years of age. When males leave, they look for a new troop to join. They usually do this by forming a bond with a female in the new troop. Unlike males, females spend their whole lives in one troop.

A big troop of baboons may break up into smaller groups during the day to **forage**. These smaller groups are made up of several females and their young, protected by a **dominant** male. Baboons can live up to 30 years in nature.

3 Weeks to 4 Years

Infants only drink their mother's milk for the first three months of their lives. At three months, the infant is able to explore on its own, eating flowers, berries, and grass. By one year, the baboon can gather almost all of its own food. At this age, a mother will start to **wean** her infant from milk.

Conservation of Baboons

Baboons can adapt quickly to different environments. Being able to cope in a wide range of habitats has helped them to survive. Of the five baboon species, only the red Guinea is considered a near **threatened** species. The red Guinea's numbers have reduced by about 25 percent since 1985. This happened as the baboon lost territory to human expansion.

After losing their territory, baboons began to enter human settlements. It is common for baboons in some parts of Africa to destroy gardens, forage in garbage bins, and even get into houses and stores in search of food. Organizations in some places, such as South Africa, employ guards to scare the baboons away from human settlements. This has reduced the conflict between animals and people.

HELPING OUT

Baboon sanctuaries house infants who have been orphaned.

Baboons take advantage of open windows to get into houses.

Myths and Legends

The ancient Egyptians had many legends about baboons. They built statues of baboons and put them in temples and tombs. The Egyptians also carved images of baboons on rocks.

To the Egyptians, the baboon represented strength. They believed that four baboons guarded the lake of fire in the underworld and judged the dead. Ancient Egyptian images often show a baboon with a scale, weighing the heart of the dead against the feather of truth. If the scale balanced, the dead person would be granted eternal afterlife.

The Egyptians believed that baboons prayed to the Sun god, Ra, each morning. The chatter of the baboons at first light was thought to be prayer. For this reason, baboons were kept as sacred animals in many Egyptian temples.

Hapi was an Egyptian god in baboon form.

Comparing Primates

This activity will help you learn more about primates and the similarities and differences between species.

Materials Needed: two pieces of paper, a pencil or pen, access to the internet

STEP 1 Research in the library and online to learn more about four different species of primate. Take note of their characteristics, such as what they look like, where they live, and what they eat.

STEP 2 Draw a picture of all four species on one of the sheets of paper. Label your drawings with the species' names.

STEP 3 Make four columns on the second sheet of paper with the four species as headings. Next, make a list of similarities and differences between these species. Do they have a tail? How large is their troop? Think about how these characteristics help each species to survive.

5 Know Your FACTS

Test your knowledge of baboons.

1 What is a group of baboons called?

2 What are baboon babies called?

3 How many species of baboon are there?

4 How large are baboon territories?

5 Where do baboons prefer to live?

Key Words

adaptations: adjustments to the natural environment

continent: one of seven divisions of land on Earth

dominant: stronger and more powerful than another animal

extinction: no longer living any place on Earth

forage: search for food

glacial periods: time during which a large part of Earth's surface was covered in ice

habitats: environments in which an animal lives

irrigation: the transportation of water to crops in areas that do not get enough water naturally

mammals: warm-blooded live-born animals that drink milk from their mother

opposable: able to touch the other fingers of the same hand or other toes of the same foot

order: in biology, a level of classification

parasites: living things that live on or inside other living things

poisonous: able to produce a harmful substance to protect itself from prey

predators: animals that hunt other animals

prey: an animal that is hunted

primates: mammals with relatively large brains, flexible hands and feet, and good eyesight

savannas: grassy plains with few trees

species: animals that share many features and can produce offspring together

threatened: in danger of no longer existing on Earth

toxic: harmful substance produced by an animal or plant

umbilical cord: a cord that supplies an unborn infant with oxygenated, nutrient rich blood

visual displays: facial expressions and gestures, such as eyebrow-raising, staring, and ground slapping

wean: to move an infant from drinking milk to eating food

Index

Log on to www.av2books.com

AV[2] by Weigl brings you media enhanced books that support active learning. Go to www.av2books.com, and enter the special code found on page 2 of this book. You will gain access to enriched and enhanced content that supplements and complements this book. Content includes video, audio, weblinks, quizzes, a slide show, and activities.

AV[2] Online Navigation

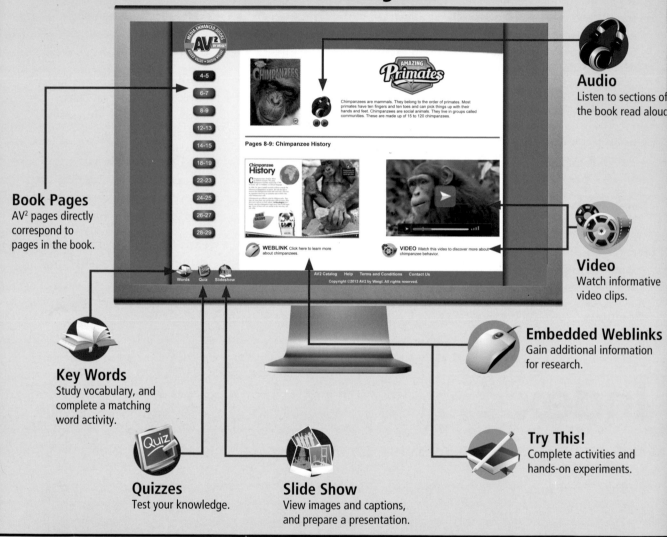

Audio
Listen to sections of the book read aloud

Book Pages
AV[2] pages directly correspond to pages in the book.

Video
Watch informative video clips.

Key Words
Study vocabulary, and complete a matching word activity.

Embedded Weblinks
Gain additional information for research.

Try This!
Complete activities and hands-on experiments.

Quizzes
Test your knowledge.

Slide Show
View images and captions, and prepare a presentation.

AV[2] was built to bridge the gap between print and digital. We encourage you to tell us what you like and what you want to see in the future.

Sign up to be an AV[2] Ambassador at www.av2books.com/ambassador.